SHERLOCK KNITS

by Joanna Johnson
Illustrated by Laurel Johnson

Slate Falls Press
Loveland, Colorado

Copyright © 2016 by Joanna Johnson

Illustrations Copyright © 2016 by Laurel Johnson

All rights reserved.

No portion of this book may be reproduced- mechanically, electronically, or by any other means, without written permission of the publisher.

Slate Falls Press, LLC

P.O. Box 7062

Loveland, CO 80537

www.slatefallspress.com

Sherlock Knits/by Joanna Johnson

ISBN 978-0-578-185446 ISBN 057818544X

Signature Book Printing, Inc.

www.sbpbooks.com

Printed in the U.S.A.

3	A SWEATER FOR JOHN
9	MRS. HUDSON'S TEA COZY
13	ELEMENTARY IN PASHMINA
17	SPECKLED BAND SHAWL
21	SOCKS FOR MARY
25	SCOTLAND YARD VEST
31	MYCROFT & MORIARTY CASEBOOK COZY
35	THE WOMAN
39	SHERLOCK HAT
43	COPPER BEECHES COWL

ABBREVIATION CHART

beg	beginning	patt	pattern
BO	bind off	pm	place marker
CO	cast on	psso	pass slipped stitch over
dec	decrease (d)	pw	purlwise
dpn	double-pointed needle	rem	remain
inc	increase (d)	rnd	round
k2tog	knit 2 together	RS	right side
k3tog	knit 3 together	sl	slip
k knit	knit	sl m	slip marker
kfb	knit in front and back of stitch	ssk	slip, slip, knit
kw	knitwise	st	stitch
m	marker	sts	stitches
m1	make one by knitting into the back of the loop just below next stitch	st st	stockinette stitch
		WS	wrong side
p	purl	wyib	with yarn in back
p2tog	purl 2 together	wyif	wyif with yarn in front
p3tog	purl 3 together	yo	yo yarn over
p2tog tbl	purl 2 together through the back loop		

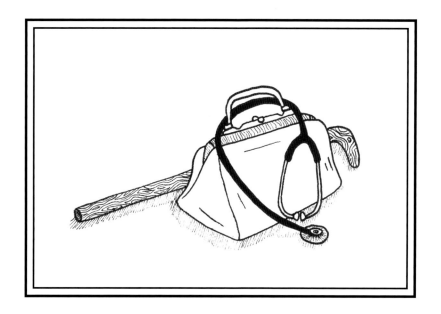

We met the next day as he had arranged, and inspected the rooms at No. 221B, Baker Street, of which he had spoken at our meeting. They consisted of a couple of comfortable bed-rooms and a single large airy sitting-room, cheerfully furnished, and illuminated by two broad windows. So desirable in every way were the apartments, and so moderate did the terms seem when divided between us, that the bargain was concluded on the spot, and we at once entered into possession.

- A Study In Scarlet

A SWEATER FOR JOHN

Finished Measurements

Sweater chest circumference measures 36 (40, 44, 48) inches 91 (102, 112, 122) cm. Shown in size 40 inches (102 cm)

Yarn

Tahki Yarns Donegal Tweed, 100% wool; 183 yards/197 meters; 100 gram skein; colorway 859 Bright Olive, 7 (8, 9, 10) skeins

Needles

US size 8 (5.0 mm) circular knitting needles 40 inches (100 cm) long

US size 8 (5.0 mm) knitting needles, short circular or double-pointed, for sleeves knit in the round

Change needle size if necessary to obtain correct gauge

Gauge

17 stitches and 23 rows = 4 inches (10 cm) in stockinette stitch pattern

Notions

Darning needle and scissors

Ten 1-inch buttons (shown: Sewology buttons #816983)

Notes

This cozy cardigan is knit seamlessly from the hem up, and includes a buttoned pocket on the right side. The body of the sweater is worked to the armpits, then put onto a holder while the sleeves are knit. The body and sleeves are then joined and worked to the neckline. Lastly, a simple garter stitch buttonhole band is picked up and knit to finish this quick and wearable sweater.

Sweater body

With longest circular needle, cast on 152 (168, 184, 200) sts and begin working back and forth.

Repeat these 10 rounds 10 times more. 58 (62, 66, 70) sts.

Work without increasing, keeping in pattern, until sleeve measures 20 inches (51 cm) or desired length.

Place all stitches on stitch holder or waste yarn to be joined to body later.

Join body and sleeves

Place first 5 and last 5 sts of each sleeve onto waste yarn or a holder for the underarm stitches.

Using longest circular needle, knit 33 (37, 41, 45) sts from the body to the first marker, remove marker, place next 10 sts on waste yarn for underarm stitches, pm, knit 19 (21, 23, 25) stitches from sleeve, sl m, p 10, sl m, k 19 (21, 23, 25) sts from rest of sleeve sts, pm, connect back of sweater by knitting 66 (74, 82, 90) sts from sweater back, place next 10 sts on waste yarn for underarm stitches, pm, knit 19 (21, 23, 25) stitches from sleeve, sl m, p 10, sl m, k 19 (21, 23, 25) sts from rest of sleeve sts, knit 33 (37, 41, 45) sts from left front of sweater. 228 (252, 276, 300) sts.

Next row: purl

Raglan shaping:

Row 1: Knit to 3 sts before first marker (marker placed between right front and sleeve), k2tog, k1, sl m, k1, ssk, knit to next marker, sl m (marker placed alongside 10 purl sts), p 10, sl m, knit to next marker (marker placed between sleeve and back), k2tog, k1, sl m, k1, ssk, knit across back to 3 sts before next marker, k2tog, k1, sl m, ssk, k to 3 sts before next marker (marker alongside 10 purl sts), p 10, sl m, k to 3 sts before next m (marker between sleeve and left front), k2tog, k1, sl m, k1, ssk, k to end of row. 8 sts dec. 220 (244, 268, 292) sts rem.

Row 2: purl

Row 3: knit across row, working 10 purl sts on each sleeve in pattern as established.

Row 4: purl

Repeat these 4 rows 4 times more. 32 sts dec. 188 (212, 236, 260) sts rem.

Begin shaping v-neck:

Keeping 4-row raglan shaping pattern as established, except:

V-neck decrease row, worked on row 1: begin row with ssk and end with k2tog, maintaining raglan decreases between. 10 sts dec. 178 (202, 226, 250) sts rem. Work remaining three rows as established.

Repeat raglan decrease and neck shaping every 4 rows 6 times more. 118 (142, 166, 190) sts rem.

Then, work neck shaping and raglan shaping decrease row every 2 rows 5 (7, 9, 10) times. 50 (70, 90, 100) sts dec. 68 (72, 76, 90) sts rem.

Knit 11 rows.

Place markers as follows: k 33 (37, 41, 45), pm, k10, pm, k 66 (74, 82, 90), pm, k10, pm, k 33 (37, 41, 45).

Begin working in pattern as follows:

Row 1: knit

Row 2: purl to m, knit to next m, purl to next m, knit to end of row

Work these two rows for 10 rows total

Place markers for pocket to be added later: knit 9 (10, 11, 12), place removable marker on next stitch, knit 18, place removable marker on next stitch, knit to the end of row

Continue as established in pattern until the body of the sweater measures 18 inches (46 cm) from cast on edge, ending after finishing a WS row. Leave all sts on needle or a holder to be joined to the sleeves later on.

Sleeves (make 2)

Using short circular or double pointed needles, cast on 36 (40, 44, 48) sts, and being careful not to twist sts, place marker and join for working in the round.

Knit 1 round, purl 1 round six times for 12 rounds total.

Place markers on next round as follows: k 13 (15, 17, 19), pm, k 10, pm, k 13 (15, 17, 19).

Begin working in pattern as follows:

Round 1: knit to m, p10, knit to end of round

Round 2: knit all sts

Repeat these two rounds three times more. (8 rounds completed).

Then, work round 1 once more.

Increase round: k1, m1, knit to last stitch, m1, k1. 38 (42, 46, 50) sts.

For sizes 36 (40, 44) only:

Next row: k2tog, k2tog, sl m, k2tog, sl m, p10, sl m, k2tog, sl m, k1, k2tog, k8 (10, 12), k2tog, k2, k2tog, k2, k2tog, k8 (10, 12), k2tog, k1, sl m, k2tog, sl m, p10, sl m, k2tog, sl m, k2tog, k2tog. 55 (59, 63) sts rem.

For size 48 only:

Next row: k2tog three times, sl m, k1, k2tog, p10, k2tog, k1, sl m, k1, k2tog, k1, k2tog, k10, k2tog, k10, k2tog, k10, k2tog, k1, k2tog, k1, sl m, k1, k2tog, sl m, k2tog, k1, sl m, k2tog three times. 74 sts rem. BO all sts pw.

Graft underarm stitches and weave in ends.

Pocket

CO 20 sts.

Sl 1 pw, knit to end.

Repeat this row until pocket measures 5½ inches (14 cm) from CO edge.

Work buttonhole

Row 1: sl 1 pw, k2, BO 2, k 10, BO 2, k 3.

Row 2: sl 1 pw, k 2, CO 2 using backward loop method, k 10, CO 2, k 3.

Next row: sl 1 pw, knit to end.

Repeat this row three times more. BO all sts.

Sew pocket to sweater as shown in the photo, using removable stitch markers to guide your placement.

Buttonband

Place markers for buttonholes: using locking stitch markers or safety pins for placement, evenly mark 8 placements for your buttons along the left front side of the sweater, beginning at the hem and ending where the v-neck shaping begins. Beginning at the right front edge of the sweater, pick up and knit stitches all along the right front side, shoulder, back of neck, left shoulder and left side, picking up 3 stitches per 4 rows along sides, and 1 stitch per stitch at shoulders and back of neck.

Knit 3 rows.

Buttonhole row 1: * knit to button marker, BO 2 sts * repeat across row, knit to end of row.

Buttonhole row 2: * knit to BO sts, CO 2 sts using backward loop method * repeat across row, knit to end of row.

Knit 2 more rows. BO all sts.

Finishing

Weave in ends. Block sweater to desired measurements. Sew 2 buttons to pocket and 8 buttons to sweater front, aligning buttons with buttonholes.

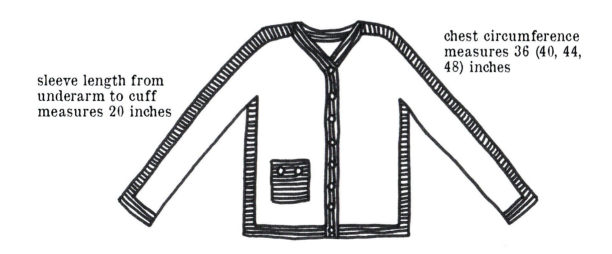

sleeve length from underarm to cuff measures 20 inches

chest circumference measures 36 (40, 44, 48) inches

"Why," said I, glancing up at my companion, "that was surely the bell. Who could come to-night? Some friend of yours, perhaps?"

"Except yourself I have none," he answered. "I do not encourage visitors."

"A client, then?"

"If so, it is a serious case. Nothing less would bring a man out on such a day, and at such an hour. But I take it that it is more likely to be some crony of the landlady's."

- The Five Orange Pips

MRS. HUDSON'S TEA COZY

Finished Measurements

To fit a standard tea pot, 6-8 inches (15-20 cm) tall and 16-18 inches (40-45cm) in circumference

Yarn

Brown Sheep Company Nature Spun Sport; 100% wool; 184 yards/168 meters; 50 gram skein

Main Color (MC), Aran, 1 skein

Contrast Color 1 (CC1), Goldenrod, 1 skein

Contrast Color 2 (CC2), Fanciful Blue, 1 skein

Needles

US size 2 (2.75 mm) double pointed knitting needles

US size 5 (3.75 mm) short (12-16 inch, 30-40 cm) circular knitting needles

Change needle size if necessary to obtain correct gauge

Gauge

24 stitches and 28 rows = 4 inches (10 cm) in stockinette stitch on larger needles

Notions

Darning needle and stitch markers

Notes

This tea cozy, inspired by "The Five Orange Pips" and decorated with colorwork orange slices, is knit in the round. To create openings for the handle and spout, steeks are cut on each side of the tea cozy. A simple two-stitch "buttonhole" opening is created on each side at the top and bottom of where the steeks are to be placed, which creates a strong finish for the openings.

Using smaller needles and MC, CO 100 sts.

Being careful not to twist stitches, place marker and join for working in the round.

Work in k2, p2 ribbing for 7 rounds total.

Switch to larger needles and work set up row: beginning of round marker, k50, place marker for side, k50 to end of round.

Please note, you will now begin working from the color chart. You will work two selvedge stitches on each side of the tea cozy to allow for the steek placement. The red line indicates where you repeat the chart on each side of the tea cozy. So, you will work 2 stitches, then, repeat the 12-stitch chart 4 times, (50 stitches); then, on the other side, you will again work 2 stitches and then repeat the chart 4 times more for your total of 100 stitches.

Rounds 1 & 2: work chart as shown.

Work steek placement opening for handle as follows:

Round 3: BO 2 sts, work chart as established to the end of the round.

Round 4: CO 2 sts using the backward loop method, work chart as established to the end of the round.

Rounds 5 & 6: work chart as established

Work steek placement opening for spout as follows:

Round 7: work as established to side marker, BO 2 sts, work to the end of the round.

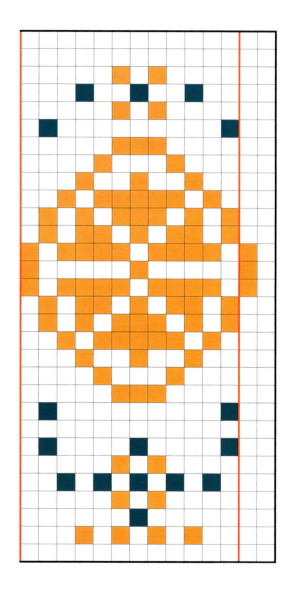

Round 8: work as established to side marker, CO 2 sts using the backward loop method, work chart as established to the end of the round.

Rounds 9-28: work chart as established

Work steek end placements as follows:

Round 29: BO 2 sts, work to side marker, BO 2 sts, work as established to the end of the round.

Round 30: CO 2 sts using the backward loop method, work to side marker, CO 2 sts using the backward loop method, work as established to the end of the round.

Switch to smaller needles and work 4 rounds in k2, p2 ribbing.

Work eyelet round: * k2, yo, k2tog * repeat from * to * across round.

Work in k2, p2 ribbing for 4 more rounds.

BO all sts loosely in pattern.

Create i-cord: using smaller needles, work a 3 stitch i-cord for 26 inches (66 cm) and secure ends.

Cut steek openings:

You have two columns of stitches between the buttonhole openings on each side of the tea cozy. The buttonhole openings mark the top and bottom of each opening where you will cut the steek.

Using your sewing machine on a short straight stitch setting, carefully stitch a straight line through the center of the first column of stitches from buttonhole to buttonhole. Repeat for the second column of stitches. This will give you space to cut your steek in the space between the stitches you have reinforced. Carefully cut steek opening; then, using a crochet hook, neatly work an edging of single crochet around the opening. Repeat for the other side.

Finishing

Weave in ends. Block tea cozy. Thread i-cord through eyelets at the top of the tea cozy.

Holmes sat in silence in the cab as we drove back to Baker Street, and I knew from his drawn brows and keen face that his mind, like my own, was busy in endeavouring to frame some scheme into which all these strange and apparently disconnected episodes could be fitted.

- The Hound of the Baskervilles

ELEMENTARY IN PASHMINA

Finished Measurements

Scarf measures 5 inches (13 cm) wide and 49 (125 cm) inches long, not including fringe

Yarn

Madelinetosh Pashmina; 75% merino, 15% silk, 10% cashmere; 360 yards/329 meters; colorway Ink, 1 skein

Needles

US size 4 (3.5 mm) knitting needles, straight or circular

Size E crochet hook for edging and fringe

Change needle size if necessary to obtain correct gauge

Gauge

26 stitches and 32 rows = 4 inches (10 cm) in stitch pattern

Notions

Darning needle and scissors

Notes

Do not be concerned if your knitting "curls" while you are knitting up this luxurious scarf. When you are done knitting, the process of blocking and edging the scarf will eliminate any curling that might take place, and the fringes lend a perfect finish.

Cast on 35 stitches and begin working in pattern.

Please use line by line instructions, as written here, or, if you prefer, use the chart provided. You will be working back and forth on 35 stitches.

Row 1: K5, * p1, k1, p1, k1, p1, k5 * repeat from * to * to end of row.

Row 2: P6, * k1, p1, k1, p7 * repeat from * to * to last 9 sts, k1, p1, k1, p6.

Row 3: work same as row 1

Row 4: work same as row 2

Row 5: work same as row 1

Row 6: * K1, p1, k1, p1, k1, p5 * repeat from * to * to last 5 stitches, k1, p1, k1, p1, k1.

Row 7: K1, p1, k1, p1, * k7, p1, k1, p1 * repeat from * to * to last stitch, k1.

Row 8: work same as row 6

Row 9: work same as row 7

Row 10: work same as row 6

Repeat these 10 rows until the scarf measures 49 inches (125 cm) from cast on edge, or work to desired length.

Bind off all stitches.

Edging

Work single crochet edging along each long side of the scarf by working in a ratio of 2 single crochet for every 3 rows of knitting to give an even finish to the edges of the scarf.

Finishing

Weave in ends. Block scarf to a tidy rectangle using a steam iron with a damp tea towel

placed between the iron and the scarf. Pin flat to dry.

Create fringe edging for the short edges of the scarf using 16-inch lengths of yarn folded once. Pull loop of yarn through the edge of the scarf from front to back, slip loop over ends of fringe and snug securely. Place one fringe for every stitch along the short sides of the scarf.

☐ RS, Knit; WS, Purl
● RS, Purl; WS, Knit

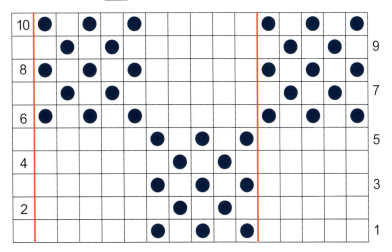

The wind was howling outside, and the rain was beating and splashing against the windows. Suddenly, amid all the hubbub of the gale, there burst forth the wild scream of a terrified woman. I knew that it was my sister's voice. I sprang from my bed, wrapped a shawl round me, and rushed into the corridor.

- The Speckled Band

SPECKLED BAND SHAWL

Finished Measurements

Shawl measures 15 inches (38 cm) from back of neck to hem, and 76 inches (193 cm) from edge to edge

Yarn

Main Color (MC): Wooly Wonka Fibers Arianrhod Sock; 75% merino, 20% silk, 5% glitter; 435 yards/398 meters; 100 gram skein; colorway Sea Dragon, 1 skein

Contrast Colors 1, 2, 3, 4 (CC1, CC2, CC3, CC4): Wooly Wonka Fibers Transitional Skein Set, Ceridwen Sock; 100% SW merino wool; 400 yards/367 meters total; colorway Fangorn Forest, 1 pack. Each skein is approximately 100 yards/91 meters. CC1 is the darkest color of the set, CC2, is the next darkest, and so forth as you progress through the shawl.

Needles

US size 5 (3.75 mm) 32 to 40 inch long circular knitting needles

Change needle size if necessary to obtain correct gauge

Gauge

24 stitches and 42 rows = 4 inches (10 cm) in garter stitch pattern

Notes

This shawl is worked from the hem to the neck edge in a combination of lace and garter stitch. The speckled yarn is alternated with bands of color from the transitional skein set, making this shawl the perfect knit for a combination of speckled and transitionally-dyed yarns.

Lace pattern, as worked back and forth over 12 rows:

Row 1: k3, * yo, k3, ssk, yo, sl 1, k2tog, psso, yo, k2tog, k3, yo, k1 * repeat from * to * across row to last 3 sts, k3.

Row 2: k3, purl to last 3 sts, k3

Row 3: work as for row 1

Row 4: k3, purl to last 3 sts, k3

Row 5: work as for row 1

Row 6: k3, purl to last 3 sts, k3

Row 7: work as for row 1

Row 8: k3, purl to last 3 sts, k3

Row 9: work as for row 1

Row 10: knit across row

Row 11: k3, purl to last 3 sts, k3

Row 12: k3, purl to last 3 sts, k3

In MC, CO 398 sts

Begin knitting back and forth, knit 2 rows

Begin working in 12 row lace pattern as follows:

In MC, work 4 rows. Pattern rows 1-4.

In CC1, work 8 rows. Pattern rows 5-12.

In MC, work 4 rows. Pattern rows 1-4.

In CC2, work 8 rows. Pattern rows 5-12.

In MC, work 4 rows. Pattern rows 1-4.

In CC3, work 8 rows. Pattern rows 5-12.

In MC, work 4 rows. Pattern rows 1-4.

In CC4, work 8 rows. Pattern rows 5-12.

In MC work 4 rows. Pattern rows 1-4.

Decrease row: in MC, * k3, k2tog* 79 times to last 3 sts, k3. 319 sts rem.

In MC, knit 3 rows. In CC1, knit 4 rows. In MC, knit 2 rows.

Decrease row: in MC, * k3, k2tog * 63 times to last 4 sts, k4. 256 sts rem.

In MC, knit 5 rows. In CC2, knit 4 rows.

Decrease row: in MC, knit 3, * k3, k2tog* 50 times to last 3 sts, k3. 206 sts rem.

In MC, knit 7 rows. In CC3, knit 2 rows.

Decrease row: in CC3, k3, * k3, k2tog * 40 times to last 3 sts, k3. 166 sts rem.

In CC3, knit 1 row. In MC, knit 6 rows.

Decrease row: in MC, k3, * k3, k2tog * 32 times to last 3 sts, k3. 134 sts rem.

In MC, knit 1 row. In CC4, knit 4 rows. In MC, knit 2 rows.

Decrease row: in MC, * k3, k2tog * 26 times to last 4 sts, k4. 108 sts rem.

In MC, knit 5 rows. In CC1, knit 2 rows.

Decrease row: in MC, * k3, k2tog * 21 times to last 3 sts, k3. 87 sts rem.

In MC, knit 7 rows.

Decrease row: in CC2, k3, * k3, k2tog * 16 times to last 4 sts, k4. 71 sts rem.

In CC2, knit 1 row. In MC, knit 6 rows.

Decrease row: in MC, k3, * k3, k2tog * 13 times to last 3 sts, k3. 58 sts rem.

In MC, knit 1 row. In CC3, knit 2 rows. In MC, knit 4 rows.

Decrease row: in MC, * k3, k2tog * 11 times to last 3 sts, k3. 47 sts rem.

In MC, knit 3 rows. In CC4, knit 2 rows.

Work the remainder of the shawl in MC.

Decrease row: * k2, k2tog * 11 times to last 3 sts, k3. 36 sts rem. Knit 1 row.

Next row: * k1, k2tog * 12 times. 24 sts rem. Knit 1 row.

Next row: * k1, k2tog * 8 times. 16 sts rem. Knit 1 row.

Next row: * k1, k2tog * 5 times, k1. 11 sts rem. Knit 1 row.

K2tog twice, k3tog once, k2tog twice. 5 sts rem.

K2tog, k1, k2tog. 3 sts rem.

K3tog. Break yarn, draw through remaining stitches to secure.

Finishing

Weave in ends. Block shawl according to your favorite method.

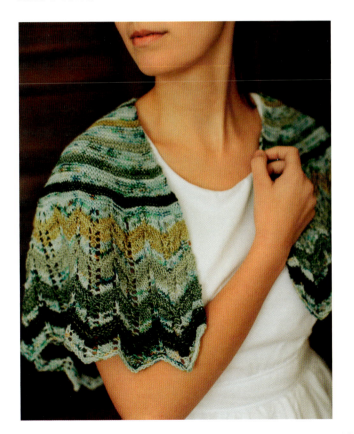

Miss Morstan and I stood together, and her hand was in mine. A wondrous subtle thing is love, for here were we two, who had never seen each other before that day, between whom no word or even look of affection had ever passed, and yet now in an hour of trouble our hands instinctively sought for each other. I have marvelled at it since, but at the time it seemed the most natural thing that I should go out to her so, and, as she has often told me, there was in her also the instinct to turn to me for comfort and protection. So we stood hand in hand, like two children, and there was peace in our hearts for all the dark things that surrounded us.

- The Sign of the Four

SOCKS FOR MARY

Yarn

Knitcircus Greatest of Ease; 80% merino, 20% nylon; 400 yards (366 meters); 100 grams; 1 (2) skeins in colorway Bears Love Honey

Needles

Size US 1 (2.25 mm) double pointed needles

Gauge

34 stitches = 4 inches (10 cm) in stockinette stitch

Size

Womens (Mens)

Cuff and foot circumference approximately 7 (9) inches; 18 (23) cm

Notes

These socks, worked over a multiple of ten stitches, are worked in the round from the cuff down using a traditional flap-style heel. You can knit the lace columns on the leg of the sock either from the line-by-line written instructions or from the chart provided.

Cast on 60 (80) sts

Being careful not to twist stitches, place marker and join for working in the round, placing 15 (20) stitches on needle 1, 15 (20) stitches on needle 2, and 30 (40) stitches on needle 3.

Leg

Begin working in lace pattern:

Work rows 1-20 of chart 3 times. Then work rows 1-6 once more.

Or, work lace pattern from line by line instructions as follows:

Rounds 1-6: K2, * p7, k3 * repeat from * to last 8 sts, p7, k1.

Round 7: * K1, yo, ssk, p5, k2tog, yo * repeat from * across round.

Round 8: K3, * p5, k5 * repeat from * across round to last 7 sts, p5, k2.

Round 9: * K2, yo, ssk, p3, k2tog, yo, k1 * repeat from * across round.

Round 10: K4 * p3, k7 * repeat from * across round to last 6 sts, p3, k3.

Round 11: * K1, (yo, ssk) twice, p1, (k2tog, yo) twice * repeat from * across round.

Round 12: K5, * p1, k9 * repeat from * across round to last 5 sts, p1, k4.

Round 13: * K2, yo, ssk, yo, sl 1, k2tog, psso, yo, k2tog, yo, k1 * repeat from * across round

Round 14: Knit all sts.

Round 15: * K3, yo, ssk, k1, k2tog, yo, k2 * repeat from * across round.

Round 16: Knit all sts.

Round 17: * K4, yo, sl 1, k2tog, psso, yo, k3 * repeat from * across round.

Round 18: Knit all sts.

Rounds 19-20: K2, * p7, k3 * repeat from * to last 8 sts, p7, k1.

Work this 20-round repeat twice more.

Work rounds 1-6 once more.

Resume working after 66 rounds are completed:

Readjust stitches for new beginning of round: K2, p3, pm for new beginning of round.

Adjust the stitches as needed, keeping the stitch count per needle as listed earlier in the pattern: 15 (20) stitches on needle 1, 15 (20) stitches on needle 2, and 30 (40) stitches on needle 3.

Next round: P4 * k3, p7 * 2 (3) times, k3, p3, k 30 (40).

Repeat this round 5 times more.

Create heel flap

Turn and work back and forth on 30 (40) sts on needle 3:

Round 1: (ws) k3, p to end

Round 2: (rs) p3, (k1, sl 1 pw wyib) 12 (17) times, end k3.

Repeat these two rows a total of 15 (20) times.

Heel turn and gusset

Set up round 1: sl1, purl 15 (20), p2tog, p1 turn

Set up round 2: sl1, k3, ssk, k1, turn

Continue working flap:

Round 1: sl1, purl to 1 stitch before the gap created on the previous row, p2tog, p1, turn

Round 2: sl1, knit to 1 stitch before the gap created on the previous row, ssk, k1, turn

Repeat these two rounds 4 (7) times more, until 18 (22) sts remain.

For smaller size only:

Next row: sl1, p to 1 st before gap, p2tog, turn.

Next row: sl1, k to 1 st before gap, ssk. 16 sts.

Resume for all sizes:

Pick up stitches along flap:

Place all 30 (40) instep stitches on one needle.

Divide heel stitches in half, placing 8 (11) stitches per needle.

Beginning of the round is now located at the center of the heel.

Needle 1: knit 8 (11), then, pick up and knit 15 (20) stitches, making sure to pick up one stitch in each garter ridge at the side of the heel flap, pick up and knit 2 stitches at the corner of the heel flap. 25 (33) stitches.

Needle 2: work across instep in established pattern. 30 (40) stitches.

Needle 3: Pick up and knit 2 stitches at the top of the left corner of the heel flap, pick up and knit 15 (20) stitches, making sure to pick up one stitch in each garter ridge at the side of the heel flap, knit 8 (11) from heel stitches. 25 (33) stitches. 80 (106) stitches total.

Work set up rounds:

Set up row needle 1: Knit to last 2 sts, ssk

Set up row needle 2: continue in pattern

Set up row needle 3: k2tog, knit to end

Begin shaping heel gusset decreases:

Round One:

Needle 1: knit to last 3 sts, k2tog, k1

Needle 2: work in pattern as established

Needle 3: k1, ssk, knit to end

Round Two:

Needle 1: knit

Needle 2: work in pattern as established

Needle 3: knit

Repeat these two rounds 8 (11) times more, needle 1 [15, (20) stitches], needle 2 [30 (40) stitches], needle 3 [15 (20) stitches]. 60 (80) sts.

Foot

Work pattern straight, keeping stockinette stitch section in place by knitting every stitch on needles 1 and 3, and keeping in pattern as established on needle 2.

Work straight until sock measures 2½ (2) inches 6 (5 cm) less than desired total length of the sock from the back of the heel.

Knit 8 rounds even.

Shape Toe

Readjust needles for toe shaping:

Knit 15 (20) sts.

Place marker for new beginning of the round.

30 (40) stitches on the top of the foot, needle 1.

15 (20) stitches for half of bottom of foot, needle 2.

15 (20) stitches for other half of bottom of foot, needle 3.

Round 1: (decrease round)

Needle 1: k1, ssk, knit to last 3 sts, k2tog, k1

Needle 2: k1, ssk, knit to end of needle

Needle 3: knit to last 3 sts on needle, k2tog, k1

Round 2: knit all stitches

Repeat these 2 rounds 7 (11) times more. 28 (32) sts rem.

Work the decrease round 3 (4) times, 12 (16) sts dec, 16 sts rem.

Place stitches from needle 2 onto needle 3.

Graft toe using kitchener stitch.

Weave in ends.

Block to desired measurements.

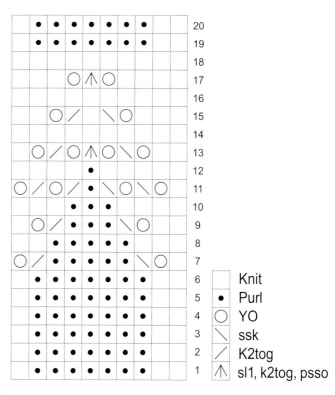

There was the clatter of running feet upon the pavement, and two policemen in uniform, with one plain-clothes detective, rushed through the front entrance and into the room.

"That you, Lestrade?" said Holmes.

"Yes, Mr. Holmes. I took the job myself. It's good to see you back in London, sir."

"I think you want a little unofficial help. Three undetected murders in one year won't do, Lestrade."

- The Adventure of the Empty House

SCOTLAND YARD VEST

Finished Measurements

Chest circumference measures 36 (40, 44, 48) inches; 91 (102, 112, 123) cm. Shown in smallest size.

Yarn

Brooklyn Tweed Loft; 100% American wool; 275 yards/251 meters; 50 gram skein

Main color (MC): Cast Iron, 3 (3, 4, 4) skeins

Contrast color 1 (CC1): Woodsmoke 2 (2, 3, 3) skeins

Contrast color 2 (CC2): Hayloft 1 skein

Needles

US size 2 (2.75 mm) 32-inch (80 cm) circular knitting needles

US size 3 (3.25 mm) 32-inch (80 cm) circular knitting needles

US size 4 (3.5 mm) 32-inch (80 cm) circular knitting needles

US size 2 (2.75 mm) 16-inch (40 cm) circular knitting needles

Size E (3.5 mm) crochet hook

Change needle size if necessary to obtain correct gauge

Gauge

26 stitches and 28 rows = 4 inches (10 cm) in stitch pattern on largest needles

Notions

Darning needle and scissors

Notes

This classic houndstooth colorwork pattern is created using stranded knitting. The colorwork chart shows that this design is created using a simple four row pattern repeat.

Be sure when choosing your yarn to select colors with a light and dark value difference. As the vest is shaped and stitches are decreased for the underarm and neckline, please remember to keep the colorwork pattern in place; the best way to do this is to follow the previous rows several stitches in as your guideline for keeping the color placement correct.

Using US size 2 (2.75 mm) 32-inch (80 cm) circular knitting needles and MC, CO 240 (264, 292, 316) sts. Being careful not to twist sts, pm and join for working in the round. Place marker at the halfway mark 120 (132, 146, 158) for the side marker.

Work in k2, p2 ribbing for 2 inches (5 cm)

Switch to US size 3 (3.25 mm) needles and CC2 and work one round of k2, p2 ribbing

Knit one round

Switch to US size 4 (3.5 mm) 32-inch (80 cm) circular knitting needles and begin working the Houndstooth colorwork pattern according to the chart, in MC and CC1. Work straight until vest measures 16 (17, 18, 19) inches; 41 (43, 46, 48) cm from the cast on edge.

Divide for armholes:

Place half of the stitches on a holder for the front, to be worked later.

Back: Keeping in pattern as established, knitting on the right side rows and purling on the wrong side rows, begin working back and forth on 120 (132, 146, 158) sts starting with the right side facing:

BO 6 (7, 8, 8) sts at the beginning of the next 2 rows

BO 4 (5, 6, 6) sts at the beginning of the next 2 rows

BO 3 (3, 3, 4) sts at the beginning of the next 2 rows

BO 2 (2, 2, 2) sts at the beginning of the next 2 rows

90 (98, 108, 118) sts rem

Continue in pattern, working back straight without shaping until it measures 8 (9, 10, 11) inches 20 (23, 25, 28) cm from the beginning of the bound off sts, ending just after finishing a wrong side row.

Shape back neck:

Continuing in color pattern as established, with right side facing, shape neck as follows:

Work 30 (32, 36, 39) sts, leave on a stitch holder, BO 30 (34, 36, 40) sts, work 30 (32, 36, 39) sts.

Turn and work on 30 (32, 36, 39) sts:

Row 1: purl across row in pattern

Row 2: ssk, knit across row in pattern. 1 st dec. 29 (31, 35, 38) sts

Repeat these 2 rows once more. 28 (30, 34, 37) sts

BO all sts knitwise.

Work other side, starting with the wrong side facing:

Row 1: purl across row in pattern

Row 2: knit across row in pattern to last 2 sts, k2tog. 1 st dec. 29 (31, 35, 38) sts

Repeat these 2 rows once more. 28 (30, 34, 37) sts

BO all sts knitwise.

Work vest front:

Keeping in pattern as established, knitting on the right side rows and purling on the wrong side rows, begin working back and forth on 120 (132, 146, 158) sts starting with the right side facing:

BO 6 (7, 8, 8) sts at the beginning of the next 2 rows

BO 4 (5, 6, 6) sts at the beginning of the next 2 rows

BO 3 (3, 3, 4) sts at the beginning of the next 2 rows

BO 2 (2, 2, 2) sts at the beginning of the next 2 rows

90 (98, 108, 118) sts rem

Divide for v-neck. Keeping in pattern, work 45 (49, 54, 59) sts, place on a holder. Work remaining 45 (49, 54, 59) sts, turn. Continue working as follows keeping in colorwork pattern:

Row 1: purl to last 2 sts, p2tog tbl

Row 2: knit

Row 3: purl

Row 4: ssk, knit to end

Row 5 purl

Row 6: knit

Repeat these six rows a total of 7 (8, 9, 10) times. 31 (33, 36, 39) sts rem.

Next row: purl to last 2 sts, p2tog tbl. 30 (32, 35, 38) sts rem.

Next row: ssk, knit to end. 29 (31, 34, 37) sts rem.

Size 36 and 40 only:

Next row: purl to last 2 sts, p2tog tbl. 28 (30) sts rem.

Size 44 and 48 only:

Next row: purl. 34 (37) sts rem.

BO all sts knitwise.

Work other side, keeping in pattern and beginning with the wrong side facing:

Row 1: p2tog, purl across row

Row 2: knit

Row 3: purl

Row 4: knit to last 2 sts, k2tog

Row 5: purl

Row 6: knit

Repeat these six rows a total of 7 (8, 9, 10) times. 31 (33, 36, 39) sts rem.

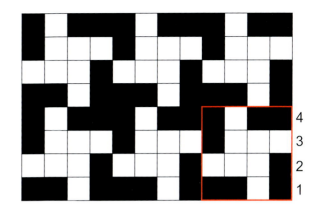

Next row: purl to last 2 sts, p2tog tbl. 30 (32, 35, 38) sts rem.

Next row: ssk, knit to end. 29 (31, 34, 37) sts rem.

Size 36 and 40 only:

Next row: purl to last 2 sts, p2tog tbl. 28 (30) sts rem.

Size 44 and 48 only:

Next row: purl. 34 (37) sts rem.

BO all sts knitwise.

Neatly sew shoulder seams using mattress stitch.

Armhole openings:

Using crochet hook method, shortest and smallest circular needles and CC1, pick up and knit 100 (108, 120, 132) sts around armhole opening.

Place marker, join for working in the round, change to CC2 and knit one round.

Work in k2, p2 ribbing for one round.

Change to MC and knit one round.

Work six rounds in k2, p2 ribbing. BO all sts.

Repeat for second armhole opening.

Neck opening:

Using crochet hook method, shortest and smallest circular needles and CC1, pick up and knit, starting at the "v" 124 (142, 154, 170) sts around neck opening.

Place marker, join for working in the round and switch to CC2. Knit one round.

Next round: k2, p2tog, p1 * k2, p2 * to last 6 sts, k2, p1, p2tog, k1. 122 (140, 152, 168) sts.

Next round: switch to MC and knit one round

Next round: k1, p2tog, * k2, p2 * to last 5 sts, k2, p2tog, k1. 120 (138, 150, 166) sts.

Next round: k1, p1, * k2, p2 * to last 4 sts, k2, p1, k1.

Next round: k1, ssk, k1, p2, * k2, p2 * to last 4 sts, k1, k2tog, k1. 118 (136, 148, 164) sts.

Next round: k3, p2, * k2, p2 * to last 3 sts, k2tog, k1. 116 (134, 146, 162) sts. BO all sts.

Finishing

Weave in ends. Block using a soak method. This yarn and stitch pattern fill out beautifully when blocked.

length from hem to armhole measures 16 (17, 18, 19) inches

chest circumference measures 36 (40, 44, 48) inches

The man pervades London, and no one has heard of him. That's what puts him on a pinnacle in the records of crime. I tell you, Watson, in all seriousness, that if I could beat that man, if I could free society of him, I should feel that my own career had reached its summit, and I should be prepared to turn to some more placid line of life.

- The Final Problem

MYCROFT & MORIARTY CASEBOOK COZY

Finished Measurements

Measures 8 inches (20 cm) wide by 10 inches (25 cm) high

Yarn

Brown Sheep Company Nature Spun Sport; 100% wool; 184 yards/(168 meters)

Colors: Charcoal, Sunburst Gold, Snow, Pepper, Scarlet, 1 skein of each color.

Needles

Size US 2 (2.75 mm) double-pointed or 16-inch (40 cm) long circular needles

Size US 5 (3.75 mm) 16-inch (40 cm) long circular needles

Gauge

24 stitches and 28 rows = 4 inches (10 cm) in stockinette stitch

Notes

This "two faced" casebook (or tablet) cozy is worked upside-down in the round, beginning with the ribbing at the top and ending with a three-needle bind-off at the bottom. Work the chart as it is printed, upside-down, so that the motifs will be right side up upon completion. For the sample shown, I used a variety of colorwork techniques, including stranded knitting, intarsia and duplicate stitching. Please use the methods you prefer, based on the patterns and numbers of colors needed per row.

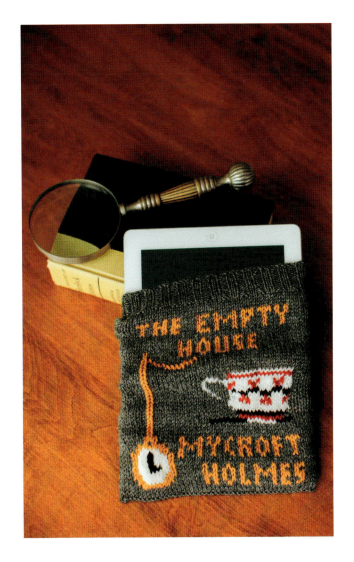

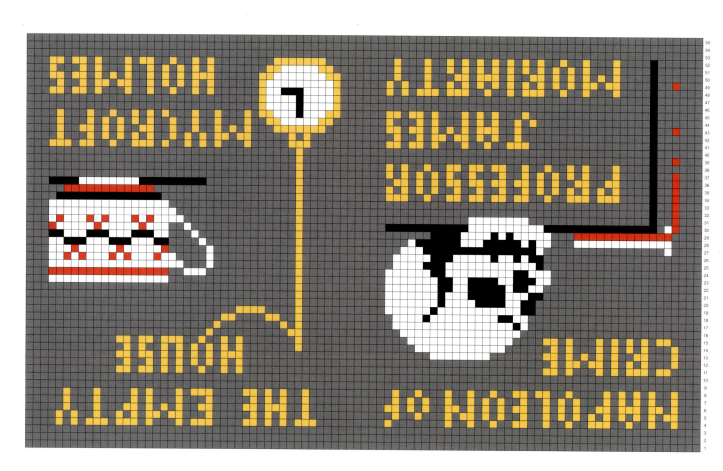

Using the smaller needles and Charcoal, CO 88 stitches. Being careful not to twist sts, place marker and join for working in the round.

Work in k2, p2 ribbing for 12 rounds.

Switch to larger needles and work increase round: k43, kfb, k43, kfb. 90 sts.

Work chart as shown, continuing in the round, using the colorwork methods of your choosing.

After you have completed the chart, put the first 45 stitches onto another needle and finish the bottom seam by working a three-needle bind-off.

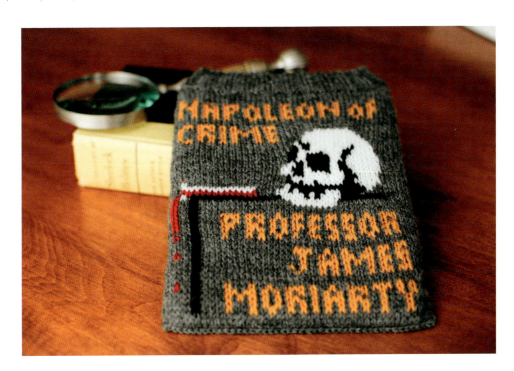

He used to make merry over the cleverness of women, but I have not heard him do it of late. And when he speaks of Irene Adler, or when he refers to her photograph, it is always under the honorable title of *the* woman.

- A Scandal in Bohemia

THE WOMAN

Size

xs (s, m, l) size shown: xs

To fit wrist circumference 6 (7, 8, 9) inches, 15 (18, 20 23) cm; bicep circumference 10 (11, 12, 13) inches, 25 (28, 30, 33) cm. 15 inches (38 cm) long after blocking.

Yarn

Lorna's Laces Helen's Lace; 50% wool, 50% silk; 1250 yards/1143 meters; 4 ounce skein; colorway Manzanita, 1/2 skein

Needles

US size 1 (2.25 mm) double-pointed knitting needles

Change needle size if necessary to obtain correct gauge

Gauge

36 stitches and 48 rows = 4 inches (10 cm) in stockinette stitch pattern

Notes

These fingerless mitts are worked in the round from the wrist up and employ a simple razor shell stitch pattern which is very stretchy and elastic once blocked. The increases are worked over the stockinette stitch panels at the beginning and end of each round, and a sturdy i-cord finger-loop is added at the end to create a fashionable finish to a simple knit.

Left/Right Mitt (make 2)

Cast on 44 (52, 60, 68) sts. Being careful not to twist sts, pm and join for working in the round.

Set up round: k2, pm, k to last 2 sts, pm, k2.

Round 1: knit to 1 st before first marker, sl 1 pw wyif, knit to second marker, sl 1 pw wyif, knit to end of round.

Round 2: knit to first marker, * yo, sl 1, k2tog, psso, yo, k1 * repeat from * to * to second marker, knit to end of round

Work these 2 rounds for 1½ inches (3.8 cm) then work increase rounds:

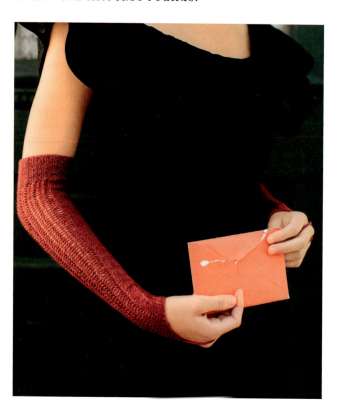

Increase round 1: knit to 2 sts before first marker, kfb, sl 1 pw wyif, knit to second marker, sl 1 pw wyif, m1, knit to end of round.

Increase round 2: knit to first marker, * yo, sl 1, k2tog, psso, yo, k1 * repeat from * to * to second marker, knit to end of round.

Continue in pattern as established, working increase round every 1½ inches (3.8 cm) 6 times more, then every ½ inch (1.25 cm) 3 times more.

Mitt now measures approximately 12 inches (30.5 cm) from cast on edge.

Change to garter ribbing stitch:

Round 1: * k2, p2 * repeat from * to * across round

Round 2: knit around

Work these two round for 1½ inches (3.8 cm)

BO all sts loosely in pattern.

Finishing

Weave in ends. Block mitts and lay flat to dry, with the beginning of the round placed at the right side for one mitt, and at the left side for the other. The stockinette stitch panels are worn along the inner elbow side of each arm. Once the mitts have dried, locate the center top of each mitt for placing the i-cord loop. Pick up 3 stitches at the center of the mitt, and using two strands of yarn held together, work i-cord for 4 inches (10 cm). Fasten off i-cord and secure to the mitt in a loop as shown. Weave in ends. Repeat for the second mitt.

Now the skillful workman is very careful indeed as to what he takes into his brain-attic. He will have nothing but the tools which may help him in doing his work, but of these he has a large assortment, and all in the most perfect order. It is a mistake to think that that little room has elastic walls and can distend to any extent. Depend upon it there comes a time when for every addition of knowledge you forget something that you knew before. It is of the highest importance, therefore, not to have useless facts elbowing out the useful ones.

- **A Study in Scarlet**

SHERLOCK HAT

Finished Measurements

To fit head circumference 22-24 inches (56-61 cm)

Yarn

Brooklyn Tweed Shelter; 100% wool; 140 yards/128 meters 50 gram skein; colorway Soot, 2 skeins

Needles

Size US 8 (5 mm) double-pointed needles

2 Size US 8 (5 mm) 16-inch (40 cm) circular needles

Gauge

20 stitches and 24 rows = 4 inches (10 cm) in stockinette stitch

Notions

Ring style stitch markers and removable (locking) stitch markers

Notes

This stylish hat, in the tradition of the classic "deerstalker" hat, has two earflaps that tie on the top, and a subtly shaped front and back brim. Knit from airy Brooklyn Tweed, it is sure to become a staple in your wardrobe. It is knit from the bottom up, and has a turned seamed hem at the bottom edge to stabilize the structure and design elements.

Cast on 90 stitches. Being careful not to twist stitches, place marker and join for working in the round. Please note: using a unique marker for the beginning of the round will help you distinguish from the other placement markers.

Knit 5 rounds.

Work purl (turning round for hem) round and place removable markers for ear flap and brim placement: purl 15, place removable marker, purl 30, place removable marker, purl 15, place removable marker, purl 30, place removable marker.

Next round: place crown shaping (ring style) markers: * knit 15, place marker * repeat 6 times. Remember to use a unique marker for the beginning of the round marker.

Begin working in slipped stitch pattern:

Round 1: * sl 1 pw wyib, knit to marker, sl marker * repeat 6 times.

Round 2: knit

Work crown shaping over next 28 rounds as follows:

Continue working rounds 1 and 2 as established, working decrease round on rounds 2, 10, 18, 22, 26 and 28 as follows:

Decrease round: * k 1, ssk, k to 2 sts before marker, k2tog * repeat 6 times across round. 12 sts decreased. Switch to double-pointed needles as necessary.

Stitch counts after rounds as follows:

After round 2: 78 sts

After round 10: 66 sts

After round 18: 54 sts

After round 22: 42 sts

After round 26: 30 sts

After round 28: 18 sts

Next round: * sl 1 pw wyib, k2tog * 6 times. 12 sts.

Next round: k2tog 6 times, removing markers as you go. 6 sts.

Cut yarn, leaving a 12 inch (30 cm) tail, draw yarn through stitches and fasten off.

Turn the hem of the hat up and to the inside of the hat at the purl round. Neatly sew hem of hat to the inside of the lower edge of the hat.

Create front brim:

In 30 sts between the removable markers, pick up sts for the brim. You will be working into the purl round. There will be two horizontal loops per each purl stitch. Using a short circular needle, pick up 30 stitches, one in each upper loop. Using a second short circular needle, pick up 30 more stitches, one in each lower loop. You will work the brim in the round on these 60 stitches, working from one needle to the next.

Join yarn and work in the round. Knit 30 stitches from upper needle and then 30 stitches from the second needle.

Repeat this 3 times more.

Decrease round: k1, ssk, k to 3 sts from end of upper stitches, k2tog, k1. Repeat for lower set of stitches.

Knit 28 from upper set of stitches, knit 28 from lower set. 56 sts total.

Repeat decrease round.

Knit 26 from upper set of stitches, knit 26 from lower set. 52 sts total.

Repeat the decrease round 7 times more. 24 sts total remain.

You will have 12 stitches on the upper set of stitches and 12 on the lower set. Graft these stitches using kitchener stitch.

Create back brim:

You will work the back brim in the remaining 30 stitches between removable markers.

You will be working into the purl round. There will be two horizontal loops per each purl stitch. Using a short circular needle, pick up 30 stitches, one in each upper loop. Using a second short circular needle, pick up 30 more stitches, one in each lower loop. You will work the brim in the round on these 60 stitches, working from one needle to the next.

Join yarn and work in the round. Knit 30 stitches from upper needle and then 30 stitches from the second needle.

Repeat this 3 times more.

Decrease round: k1, ssk, k to 3 sts from end of upper stitches, k2tog, k1. Repeat for lower set of stitches.

Knit 28 from upper set of stitches, knit 28 from lower set. 56 sts total.

Repeat decrease round.

Knit 26 from upper set of stitches, knit 26 from lower set. 52 sts total.

Repeat the decrease round 5 times more. 32 sts total remain.

You will have 16 stitches on the upper set of stitches and 16 on the lower set. Graft these stitches using kitchener stitch.

Side flaps (make 2):

Pick up 15 stitches in the upper purl ridge between removable markers. You will start working with the wrong side (inside of hat) facing you.

Row 1: sl 1 pw wyib, knit to end of row

Row 2: sl 1 pw wyif, purl to end of row

Repeat these two rows 9 times more

Decrease row: sl 1 pw wyib, ssk, knit to last 3 sts, k2tog, k1. 13 sts.

Next row: sl 1 pw wyif, purl to end of row

Work another decrease row. 11 sts.

Next row: sl 1 pw wyif, purl to end of row

Work another decrease row. 9 sts.

Next row: sl 1 pw wyif, p2tog, p3, p2tog tbl, p1. 7 sts.

Next row: sl 1 pw wyib, ssk, k1, k2tog, k1. 5 sts.

Next row: sl 1 pw wyif, p3tog, p1. 3 sts.

Using double pointed needles, work i-cord for 10 inches (25 cm) on the remaining 3 stitches. Cut yarn and draw through stitches, fasten off.

Finishing

Weave in ends. Block.

I could see that Holmes was favorably impressed by the manner and speech of his new client. He looked her over in his searching fashion, and then composed himself, with his lids drooping and his finger-tips together, to listen to her story.

- The Adventure of the Copper Beeches

COPPER BEECHES COWL

Finished Measurements

Cowl measures 17 inches (43 cm) high and 50 inches (127 cm) in circumference. Please note these measurements are after blocking. Pre-blocking measurements are 15 inches (38 cm) high and 40 inches (102 cm) in circumference.

Yarn

Blue Sky Fibers Techno; 68% baby alpaca, 10% extra fine merino, 22% silk; 120 yards/109 meters; 50 gram skein; colorway Fame, 4 skeins

Needles

US size 10½ (6.5 mm) 32 inch (80 cm) long circular knitting needles

Change needle size if necessary to obtain correct gauge

Gauge

12 stitches and 18 rows = 4 inches (10 cm) in stitch pattern

Notions

Darning needle and scissors

Notes

This cloud-like cowl is worked in the round with a simple two-row stitch pattern. The slipped stitch is carried across the front of the knitting, creating horizontal stitch movement along the lace fabric.

Cast on 141 stitches

Being careful not to twist stitches, place marker and join for working in the round.

Knit 1 round

Purl 1 round

Knit 1 round

Purl 1 round

Knit 1 round

Begin working in openwork lace pattern:

Round 1: * yo, slip 1 stitch purlwise with yarn in front, k2, pass slipped stitch over the two knit stitches * repeat from * to * across round

Round 2: knit

Repeat these two rounds until you have about 35 yards (32 meters) of yarn remaining, or to desired size.

Knit 1 round

Purl 1 round

Knit 1 round

Purl 1 round

Knit 1 round

BO all stitches

Finishing

Weave in ends. Block cowl using a soak method.

Deepest thanks to:

Laurel Johnson, for her beautiful artwork, for modeling, and also for being my creative sounding board. www.mountainlaurelartwork.com

Christa Tippmann, for her amazing photographs, artistry, and moral support. www.christatippmannphotography.com

Hadley Austin, my tech editor, for her attention to detail, patience, and wisdom.

Stephanie Flynn Sokolov, for her constant encouragement.

Karen DeGeal, for her beautiful sample knitting and invaluable feedback.

Megan Helzer, my copy editor, for graciously pointing out my many mistakes.

Joyce Bensen, my mom, for her helpfulness in test knitting.

Alan and Judy Johnson, for the use of their beautiful home.

Jason Hurd, for the loaning of his nifty tobacco pipe.

Our models: Jonathan Grimm, Laurel Johnson, Caleb Mackoy, and Benjamin and Bex Wishart; you were all enthusiastic, patient, and wonderful.

Don Pierson, owner of Dickens Alley in Loveland, Colorado, for allowing us to do photography in his incredible shop: Dickens Alley, Rare Books, Art & Antiques 238 East 4th Street Loveland, CO 80537

(970) 667-9333 Open 10-6 Monday-Saturday dickensalley@comcast.net

The yarn companies who generously provided yarns for the patterns in this book: Blue Sky Fibers, Brooklyn Tweed, Brown Sheep Company, Knitcircus Yarns, Lorna's Laces, Madelinetosh, Tahki Stacy Charles, and Wooly Wonka Fibers.

My husband and book designer, Eric, and our three wonderful children, for their love and support, and the joy and meaning they bring to my life. To God, for loving and guiding me.